THE
POSITIVITY
COACH

A Pocket Coach

THE
POSITIVITY
COACH

GILL THACKRAY

Michael O'Mara Books Limited

This book is dedicated to Viv Dutton, my twin sister, for a lifetime's supply of encouragement, support, positivity and coffee.

First published in Great Britain in 2020 by
Michael O'Mara Books Limited
9 Lion Yard
Tremadoc Road
London SW4 7NQ

A CIP catalogue record for this book is available from the British Library.

Papers used by Michael O'Mara Books Limited are natural, recyclable products made from wood grown in sustainable forests. The manufacturing processes conform to the environmental regulations of the country of origin.

ISBN: 978-1-78929-253-4 in hardback print format
ISBN: 978-1-78929-255-8 in ebook format

2 3 4 5 6 7 8 9 10

www.mombooks.com
Follow us on Twitter @OMaraBooks

Cover and design by Ana Bjezancevic
Typeset by Claire Cater

Printed and bound in China

CONTENTS

▼▼▼

INTRODUCTION

As human beings, we have evolved with the biological imperative to survive. This means that we are 'hardwired' to look for threat and danger. Our negativity bias may have kept us safe from predators once upon a time, but in modern-day life it can be counterproductive. Scientists are beginning to understand how negative emotions, instead of protecting us, can take an enormous toll on our mental wellbeing and physical health. Negativity keeps us stuck in mental habits that limit our growth and our opportunities in life.

It's normal to recognize negativity in your own life. We are all capable of negative thoughts. This might be our default response, but there is another way of approaching the world. A way that is more effective and comes with a plethora of psychological, cognitive, emotional and physical benefits. Positivity is a mindset, or perspective on life. The good news? We can train our brains to respond in a positive way.

Developing a more positive perspective of the world is a way of mitigating against what can sometimes feel like an onslaught of negativity. Positivity isn't about wishful thinking. It doesn't mean embracing a bumper-sticker approach to life, or ignoring reality. Think of it as developing a glass-half-full approach to life that energizes you and keeps you alive to opportunities, rather than being bogged down with a worldview that skews your every perception.

While we can't prevent bad things from happening to us, we can choose how we respond. Cultivating more positivity in your life will increase your ability to manage negative life events. You'll find that you're better able to focus on the present moment, to manage your emotions and focus on solutions, rather than dwelling on the problem.

Psychologist Kendra Cherry describes positivity as 'approaching life's challenges with a positive outlook. It does not necessarily mean avoiding or ignoring the bad things; instead, it involves making the most of the potentially bad situations, trying to see the best in other people, and viewing yourself and your abilities in a positive light.'

How we think has a huge impact upon how we relate to the world. It influences our relationships with others, the goals that we set ourselves, what we feel capable of achieving, our self-esteem, and even our resilience when things don't go to plan.

Pause for a moment and consider the areas of your life where you would like to make positive changes. Is there something that you've always wanted to accomplish but shied away from? A dream that you've shelved? Are there areas that you would like to develop, but you don't know how? If we remain stuck in negative thinking patterns, we might never try. With a more positive outlook we can begin to disrupt that habitual thinking. We can become more receptive to new information that will help us. When we adopt a more positive attitude, we're less afraid of failing because we know we have the tools to learn from failure. We can become unstuck. Those accomplishments become more possible with a positive mental attitude. Positivity is about developing the grit to push through your self-limiting beliefs, creating the mental resources to help you move forward – in a direction that you choose.

Scientists have been studying positive emotions since the 1950s. In a move away from the traditional focus of pathology, psychology developed a new branch to examine what is happening when human beings live positively and flourish. Positive psychology is the scientific study of how people thrive and promote positivity in their everyday lives. Psychologist Martin Seligman describes this approach as 'building what's strong' instead of 'fixing what's wrong'. It complements rather than replaces traditional psychology, providing us with an empirical road map for positivity. Positive psychology is now used in a variety of fields, including sports psychology, business, coaching and education to optimize performance and wellbeing.

A positive outlook forms the building blocks of belief in yourself, your unique gifts and abilities. Embracing a positive attitude won't guarantee happiness but it will help you to develop confidence in your own abilities, to approach challenges more effectively and manage difficult situations with skill. Positivity is a habit that you can develop and strengthen using science-backed strategies.

Like any skill, cultivating positivity takes time, effort and practice – until it becomes a habit. The results, for you and for those around you, will be worth the effort. Committing to positivity will equip you with a valuable life skill and the personal resources to live a happy and fulfilled life.

▲ ▲ ▲

ACCESSING
the power of
POSITIVITY

The science of happiness reveals that there are enormous physical and psychological benefits when we adopt a positive outlook. Psychologists studying the impact of positivity have discovered that a positive attitude is linked to:

- Reduced stress and anxiety

- Increased longevity

- A greater sense of wellbeing

- Cardiovascular health

- Lower incidence of depression

- Greater resilience

- More motivation

- Higher levels of energy

- Improved relationships

- Increased general happiness

Positivity is the ability to navigate whatever the world throws at you with optimism. Unfortunately, that's not the way we are built. Our brains have evolved with a negativity bias which scans everything for threats in order to keep us from harm. It's an ancient mechanism that kept us vigilant against predators, but can sometimes hold us back.

Positive thinking isn't about promoting a false feel-good state. Neither does it require you to deny reality. The opposite is true. A positive attitude is an essential set of skills that will enable you to identify faulty negative thinking. You'll begin to see where you are impeding your own progress. Positivity provides a framework to help you fulfil your potential and achieve your goals.

If positive thinking isn't your natural outlook on life, you can cultivate it by adopting a range of simple, practical strategies. Think of it as building a new habit, a way of retraining your mind to break old negative, unhelpful patterns.

ISN'T POSITIVITY JUST BEING ANNOYINGLY CHEERFUL?

You could be forgiven for thinking that positivity is all about being in denial – to some people, that might be how it looks. This is known as 'toxic positivity'. Viewing positivity through that lens is misleading, though. Genuine positivity isn't about pretending that all is well in the world when it isn't. It's about recognizing what doesn't work and changing it, on an individual and societal level. Developing positivity means that you have a toolkit of techniques, strategies and practices that will buffer any stressful events in life that you encounter.

PRIMING YOUR BRAIN FOR POSITIVITY

Every single thought that we generate has an impact upon our physiology. Negative, stressful thoughts release a hormone called cortisol into the body. Cortisol itself isn't a bad thing. It has many useful functions, including reducing inflammation, helping to manage our blood sugar levels and controlling blood pressure. You might already know it as the hormone that is responsible for the 'fight, flight, freeze' response in your body. Cortisol keeps us safe when we are in immediate danger. It helps us to survive.

Unfortunately, when cortisol hangs around in our body for too long, too often, it can begin to cause problems. That's when we start to notice that things which are not an immediate threat to our survival – such as being late, getting stuck in traffic, anxious thoughts, or arguing with someone – also elicit the 'fight, flight or freeze' response, and that's unhelpful. We've probably all experienced that kind of stress. It becomes a cycle of constant high alert. Stress that doesn't go away becomes chronic and harmful. Priming your brain for positivity, then, begins with your thoughts and the ability to catch anxious, stressful thoughts early, before they can get out of control. A happy brain is a more effective brain. It can think more clearly, be more creative and is better at problem-solving.

◆ WHY POSITIVITY MATTERS ◆

Research shows that when you practise positivity, you are safeguarding your mental health. It's a way of training your brain that builds your confidence, creating a sense of self-efficacy – the knowledge that you *know* you can cope with whatever life throws at you. Studies also show that positive mental training has significant health benefits. It reduces your stress levels, decreases anxiety and burnout while at the same time building resilience. It doesn't stop there: positivity can also help us to manage the physical symptoms of stress – for example, headaches, fatigue and chronic pain.

◆ THE MIND, BODY, POSITIVITY CORRELATION ◆

We talked about the impact of cortisol on our bodies and the link between stress and our perception. When we think positive, optimistic, happy thoughts we can begin to shift our perception, creating a happier state. This enables your nerve cells to produce serotonin, a neurotransmitter that sends messages from one part of your brain to another. Serotonin is important for brain function, to regulate mood, wellbeing and happiness. Positivity can help us to get more of it.

◆ POSITIVITY FOR CYNICS ◆

Perhaps you're reading this and feeling more than a bit cynical? Maybe you're wondering if positivity really works or if it really makes any tangible difference in life. That's okay. We can and should question the evidence when new information is presented to us. Cynicism isn't always a negative trait, but some studies suggest that cynics may have a higher rate of cardiovascular disease and dementia. I'd encourage you to examine the science behind positivity. It's a great place to start if you are looking for evidence that developing positivity works – spoiler alert, it does.

◆ LOCUS OF CONTROL ◆

Developing your locus of control can have a considerable impact upon your life. Identified in the 1950s by psychologist Julian Rotter, it is an important aspect of your personality. It shapes everything from your positivity to your resilience and the way that you manage stress. Locus of control refers to your efficacy, or how capable you feel when things happen to you. It is best viewed as a spectrum, rather than wholly external or internal.

An internal locus of control means that you believe you have power over external life events. You believe that your actions can influence and shape those events. Picking up this book and being willing to try some of the positivity exercises suggests that you have at least some internal locus of control.

If you have an external locus of control you believe that external forces determine your life events and that there is very little that you can do to change that. An external locus of control may prevent you from changing any of your current habits because you don't believe it will make any difference.

Generally, strengthening your internal locus of control will help you to manage stress and build resilience. Reflect for a moment upon how you perceive your ability to be proactive when it comes to resilience. Do you consider yourself to have an external or internal locus of control?

If you recognize more of a predisposition towards external, you can begin to change that. Here's how:

1. **Recognize that you have a choice.** You can always choose how you respond to external events. Monitor your self-talk and replace 'I must...' with 'I choose to...'.

2. **Focus on what you can control.** Instead of placing your focus on what you can't control, zone in on what you can influence and control instead.

3. **Brainstorm ideas.** When you're faced with a challenge, get as many ideas as you can, either generated by you or other people that you trust. Don't judge ideas as good or bad initially, be open to all of them. See how many options

you can come up with and then sift. Evaluate the best course of action for you.

- -

Practical exercise

Audit your thoughts

It's important to know what your baseline is in terms of your positivity. See if it's possible to monitor your thoughts for the next twenty-four hours. Are you able to recognize a pattern? You might be surprised: some thoughts can last for less than a second and it's not until we really begin to pay attention to them that we are able to identify negative patterns that creep in throughout the day. If it helps, keep a record of what you notice. Are there any emerging themes? Do you notice anything – an external locus of control in some areas, for example – that you'd like to work on and change?

- -

▲▲▲

REWIRING YOUR BRAIN

for

POSITIVITY

POSITIVE NEUROSCIENCE: ✦ A NEW WAY OF LOOKING AT ✦ HUMAN FLOURISHING

We used to think that what we were born with, we were stuck with, where our brains are concerned – that everything was 'fixed' from birth. With the advent of neuroscience, we now know that's not true. We have discovered that our thoughts can actually change our brain, in a process that's known as neuroplasticity.

NEUROPLASTICITY: ✦ HOW YOUR EXPERIENCE ✦ SHAPES YOUR BRAIN

Your brain is able to change continuously by forming new connections and pathways. This process is known as neuroplasticity. Your brain has the ability to reroute neural circuits and grow new neurons (neurogenesis). This is a lifelong process. Our brains are truly amazing in the way that they transform in response to our experiences.

Every single thought or emotion that we have, positive or negative, reinforces a neural network. Each thought leads to tiny changes in our brain when repeated frequently. Think of these neural networks as roads. The more we use them, the stronger and wider they get, creating superhighways. When we don't use them, they become narrow and restricted, like an overgrown country road. Over time, the thoughts we repeat most become automatic and, eventually, part of the way we are. We become what we think and do on a regular basis. It makes sense, then, that we would want to cultivate positivity.

◆ REWIRING YOUR BRAIN ◆

Now we know that we can reshape and rewire our brains, how do we go about it? World-renowned neuropsychologist Donald Hebb's principle that the neurons that fire together, wire together is our starting point. When you recognize that your thinking is less than positive, don't blame yourself. Our habits are formed at an early age, before we're even aware of them.

The good news is that you can change. One of the ways to rewire your brain is to become aware of when you are experiencing a positive emotion. That's not always as easy as it might sound.

Neuroscience has shown that positive experiences tend to evaporate. They're not stored in our robust, long-term memory in the same way that negative experiences are. Psychologist Rick Hanson argues that we can rewire this innate mechanism by consciously taking in the good. He says that we can begin to hardwire ourselves for happiness by making time, every day, to take in good things. To store those positive emotions, we need to hold onto them for between twelve and twenty seconds.

The next time you see an awesome view, something makes you smile or you experience a positive emotion, take the time to allow it to sink in. Savour it for between twelve and twenty seconds. The more you do this, the more you are programming yourself to look for positivity.

▲▲▲

HOW POSITIVITY STRENGTHENS RESILIENCE

Barbara Fredrickson, a professor of psychology, discovered that positivity is one of the key traits of happy people. Fredrickson found that when we view challenging life events with curiosity, openness and positivity, we are better placed to manage them. Even better, when we cultivate positivity, the benefits are long-lasting.

Fredrickson advises increasing your 'daily diet' of emotions and within three months you'll begin to see a shift to a more positive, resilient, connected self.

Think of developing positivity rather than forcing it. There will be times that you don't feel positive and that's okay – you're human. Forcing positivity can be counterproductive, leaving us feeling worse than when we started. Aim to develop your positivity every day, little by little, and you'll begin to rewire your brain.

◆ BOOSTING YOUR ◆ MENTAL HEALTH

The World Health Organization's (WHO) definition of health highlights positivity when it comes to mental health: 'Health is a state of complete physical, mental and social well-being and not merely the absence of disease or infirmity.'

Practising positivity has been linked to improved mental health. That doesn't mean that bad things won't happen or that you'll no longer notice them. What it does mean is that you'll feel more in control and better placed to manage them when they do come along.

◆ SUBJECTIVE WELLBEING (SWB) ◆

How we interpret our world hugely influences our subjective wellbeing, or how good we feel about life. Professor Ed Diener, known as 'Dr Happiness', discovered that although there is no single secret ingredient to happiness, people who were very happy had rich social relationships and spent little time alone. We talk more about cultivating these kinds of satisfying relationships in 'Positivity and Relationships' (see pages 57–68). It's also possible to develop high subjective wellbeing by increasing the number of times that you experience positive states.

Diener found that subjective wellbeing is an important ingredient for individuals, communities and society overall. It affects our quality of life, happiness, mental health – and has even been linked to the GDP of countries.

Positive thinking helps you to identify the areas that you want to change. You're better able to focus and feel more encouraged to set goals so that you can change situations that don't work for you.

◆ CREATING SPACE FOR AWE ◆ AND POSITIVE EMOTIONS

We know from research that positive emotions are associated with a number of benefits for our health and wellbeing. Positive emotions can help us to maintain good physical health.

Awe is a huge component of positivity. Once you begin to look for awe, you'll discover it everywhere. In a sunset, playing with pets, when someone is smiling at you, or time spent in nature.

Researchers at the University of California, Berkeley, found that positive emotions such as joy, awe, pride, amusement and love reduced inflammation within the body. Of all of those positive emotions, awe reduced levels of interleukin-6 – the molecule most associated with inflammation.

$\cdot$ $\cdot$ $\cdot$ $\cdot$ $\cdot$ $\bullet$ $\bullet$ $\bullet$ $\bullet$ $\bullet$ $\bullet$ $\bullet$ $\bullet$ $\bullet$ $\bullet$ $\bullet$ $\bullet$ $\cdot$ $\cdot$ $\cdot$ $\cdot$

Practical exercise

Experiencing awe

Reflect on the last time that you experienced awe. Where were you? What was happening? Are you able to hold that image in your mind and let it soak in?

At the beginning of each day, set an intention to build awe into your day. Think about how you can create the opportunity to experience awe. You might not be able to go and visit a majestic mountain or stunning seascape, but think about producing micro-moments of awe. Can you source videos, images or sounds that evoke awe for you? Begin to build these into your routine until you are actively seeking awe every day.

◆ MENTAL REHEARSAL ◆

Neuroplasticity can take place without you having to move a muscle. Your brain doesn't know the difference between imagining something and it taking place in real time. When you mentally rehearse something, or recall from memory, your brain will still experience plasticity-based learning. This is a technique often used in sports psychology to improve performance and achieve personal bests.

Try it. From memory or imagining something new,

run through the thing that you would like to achieve. For example: if you would like a new job, visualize yourself going for the interview. See it as though you are looking through a camera lens, rather than watching yourself. Picture the interview going exactly how you would like it to go. The panel are impressed with your answers. You feel confident. Then visualize yourself receiving the job offer. Or you might have another goal, one around health or fitness.

The best time to do this is first thing in the morning, just after waking, and last thing at night before sleep. This is when your brain is in the alpha state, our most relaxed default state, when our mind is clear of mental clutter and we're more receptive to this type of visualization.

▲▲▲

MASTERING

negative

THOUGHTS

◆ RECOGNIZING YOUR ◆
INNER CRITIC

Your negative inner critic is easily identified. You'll know it by its lack of support and unwillingness to see the good in anything. Think of it as an emotional vampire. We all have one. Our inner narrative can be non-stop or every now and again. It consists of the things that we don't necessarily say out loud and is a mix of our unconscious assumptions and beliefs. It has the potential to be positive or negative, but for many people it's overwhelmingly critical.

The volume varies but the script is usually the same: 'You're not good enough', 'People will think that you're stupid', with words like 'should', 'must' and 'have to' littered among its advice. It reveals some of our beliefs about ourselves that operate on a subconscious level. Although that internal critic might be imperceptible and barely audible at times, it's important to remember that words are powerful.

That internal voice guides our perception of the world. What we say (or don't say) to ourselves impacts our behaviour and our performance along with our happiness. Self-talk can amplify our limiting self-beliefs, but there is an alternative. We can create a new self-talk that motivates, encourages and inspires us.

Recognizing your inner monologue is the starting point for changing it from self-defeating chatter to something more positive. With practice, you'll get better at noticing it.

◆ UNDERSTANDING NEGATIVE ◆ SELF-TALK AND THOUGHTS

When your self-talk is mainly negative, it feeds into feeling bad about yourself. We've talked about neuroplasticity and rewiring your brain; negative monologues continue to wire us for – you've guessed it – negativity. It also has a negative impact upon our health.

▲▲▲

◆ HOW POSITIVE SELF-TALK ◆ AFFECTS YOUR HEALTH

Research has shown that positive self-talk can:

- Reduce symptoms of anxiety and depression

- Increase self-esteem

- Improve mood

- Result in a more positive body image

◆ MONITORING YOUR SELF-TALK ◆

You may not even be aware of your self-talk. Make an effort to monitor it for the next twenty-four hours. See what you notice: is it constant chatter? Only vocal every now and again or does it seem to happen for less than a second each time that you hear it? Are there patterns? Do you notice themes emerging around specific areas of your life?

Once you begin to notice your self-talk, you might be surprised at what you discover. You may find that you are focusing only on the negative. Perhaps you are exaggerating things, or being unreasonable to yourself. Sometimes our thinking is faulty, biased towards what isn't working, rather than what is. Because we've never brought our awareness to it, we just haven't noticed. Many of us have no idea that we are being quite so harsh with ourselves on a regular basis. As you monitor your self-talk, ask yourself if you would speak to a friend in the same way, to gain some perspective.

◆ REFRAMING NEGATIVE EVENTS ◆

There are some quick and effective ways to test out your negative thinking. Begin by asking yourself some probing questions.

▲▲▲

◆ WHERE'S THE EVIDENCE? ◆

Ask yourself, 'Am I 100 per cent sure that this is true? Where is the evidence?' Your thoughts may not be accurate. Is there evidence that suggests you are wrong in your assumptions about the situation?

◆ ALTERNATIVE EXPLANATIONS ◆

'Is this simply my interpretation of what's happening? Is there another way of looking at this?' Looking for alternative explanations can be a helpful way of reframing those negative thoughts. For example, you didn't get a promotion you wanted. You believe, 'I'm useless at what I do. I'll never get the job I really want.' You can reframe this scenario to, 'I'll get feedback from the interview and work on those areas.'

▲▲▲

◆ PERSPECTIVE-TAKING ◆

By asking yourself a series of key questions, you can gain perspective on difficult situations and be better placed to meet challenges as they arise.

Is this really as bad as I think it is?

· · • • ●

What's the worst thing that could happen here?

● • • · ·

What's the best thing that could happen for me in this situation?

· · • • ●

What's most likely?

● • • · ·

Will it matter in a year's time?

◆ POSITIVE MINDSET ◆

Instead of engaging in a downward spiral of thinking, questions posed from a positive mindset enable you to move out of stress response into a more useful, resilient mindset.

How can I change my thinking
to help me in this situation?

● ● ● · ·

What can I learn from this?

· · ● ●

What's the best way for me to
overcome this?

● ● ● · ·

What could I do differently next time?

▲ ▲▲

OVERCOMING
◆ WEAPON-FOCUS THINKING ◆

A negative outlook that takes hold and refuses to budge is known as weapon-focus thinking. The term originates from the behaviour of people held at gunpoint, experiencing heightened anxiety and stress. It's a sharp focus of perception that seeks out negative information. When you're in the grip, you can begin to see how weapon focus became a way of describing a pattern of extreme negative thinking. It's important to remember that these thoughts are just thoughts. It is possible to create an upward cycle by creating positive emotions instead.

◆ CREATING POSITIVE EMOTIONS ◆

By looking for opportunities to increase the amount of positivity in your life, you can create positive momentum. Think of positivity as a way of reversing the downward spiral that we often experience when we have a low mood. Psychologists at the University of California asked participants to write each week, focusing on specific topics. One group wrote about positive events that they were grateful for each week. The other group wrote about things that had irritated them. The group focusing on positive experiences reported feeling more optimistic, experiencing increased wellbeing. They also had better health and fewer visits to their doctor than the group focusing on irritations. Positivity psychologists have discovered that it's possible to create positive emotions.

Practical exercise

A letter of thanks

Is there someone in your life who has supported you? A pivotal person who has made a huge difference to you, but doesn't know it? Perhaps someone who you have never thanked before? Write a letter, or an email, expressing your thankfulness for their kindness and send it. Studies at the University of Pennsylvania found that when people wrote letters of gratitude they experienced an enormous increase in their level of happiness. What's more, the benefits of this intervention lasted for an entire month. You'll also be paying your gratitude forward by letting someone else know how much their support has meant to you.

Mental thank yous

If you are no longer able to thank someone for their help, inspiration or support, send them a mental thank you instead.

Blessings audit

Make time each week to focus on the things that have gone well for you. Count your blessings by writing them down. Try to visualize in detail the things that you are grateful for each week. Describe them vividly. If it helps, pick a number of things that you will write about: for example, ten blessings each week. You can do this daily, if you choose to.

▲▲▲

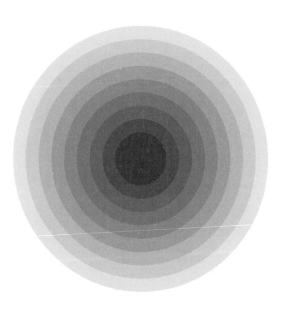

USING POSITIVITY
to build
CONFIDENCE & SELF-BELIEF

◆ THE SECRET OF ◆
SELF-CONFIDENCE

Self-confidence is how we perceive ourselves: the opinion that we have of ourselves, either positive or negative. Our beliefs about ourselves and our capabilities contribute towards our overall confidence. Self-confidence is pivotal when it comes to achieving your goals and developing a more positive outlook on life.

You might find that in some areas of life your confidence is high, while in others it might be low. It's normal to doubt your ability from time to time and we all experience those moments. If, however, you find that you are constantly questioning yourself and your abilities, it can affect your mental health and wellbeing. If you recognize low self-confidence, developing positivity can play an important part in raising confidence and self-esteem.

▲▲▲

◆ IMPOSTER SYNDROME AND ◆ HOW TO OVERCOME IT

Imposter syndrome is the feeling that you just don't deserve your success. It's characterized by the belief that your accomplishments are pure luck. What's more, it's peppered with that awful feeling that you'll be found out. If it sounds familiar, one in seven of us will experience it at some point. It's surprisingly commonplace, especially when, if you have it, you assume nobody else does.

Imposter syndrome shakes our self-confidence and prevents us from going for what we want. If you've shunned or discounted the possibility of promotion because you don't think that you're good enough, or shelved a goal because, well, you'll never achieve it, then you've experienced imposter syndrome.

The quickest way to overcome imposter syndrome is to feel that anxiety around trying something new, set a goal anyway and go for it. Do the things that scare you. Monitor your progress along the way, recognizing and celebrating what you've learned.

◆ DEVELOPING SELF-ACCEPTANCE ◆

Sometimes, we can be our own harshest critic. Perhaps, when you began to monitor your self-talk, you realized that? Or maybe you recognized that you would never, ever speak to a friend the way that you regularly speak to yourself? We waste an enormous amount of time beating ourselves up for not being good enough, for what we don't have, or can't do. It's misplaced energy that can derail us.

Self-acceptance involves becoming more aware of your strengths and weaknesses, and accepting them all. Right here, right now. It doesn't depend upon becoming thinner, better looking or more intelligent. Sometimes self-acceptance can feel tenuous, or fluid. Easy on a good day, trickier when things haven't gone as planned, or we feel that we've messed up in some way. Self-acceptance is something that we need to nurture, regularly.

Sometimes this means peeling away the layers and taking a gentle look at the areas that we might ordinarily avoid. It's not easy to look at the parts of ourselves that we don't like very much. Making friends with our less appealing parts can help to alleviate self-criticism, self-doubt and our self-defeating beliefs. Being able to like ourselves, all of ourselves, unconditionally, is critical for self-acceptance.

Unconditional self-acceptance rests upon the understanding that you are separate from your actions. We're all flawed, it's part of being human. It's also what makes us unique.

◆ THERE'S ONLY ONE YOU ◆

It may sound like pop psychology but there really is only one you. You're unique. All of you. The parts of yourself that you like and the parts of yourself that you don't. Healthy self-esteem means recognizing that you are a work in progress. Self-esteem researcher Morris Rosenberg describes it as a 'favourable or unfavourable attitude toward the self'. It's how we view ourselves; our sense of worth in the world.

When we have low self-esteem, we focus upon our mistakes and failures, sometimes exaggerating them. That makes it difficult to progress or to improve, and can lead to pessimism, depression and poorer life outcomes. We can easily get stuck when we narrow our focus to the negatives unless we consciously do something different.

It's not your fault if you recognize yourself in this description. Low self-esteem is multi-factorial and dependent upon a number of variables, including:

- Your life experiences

- Self-talk

- Genes

- Representations in the media

- Personality

- Age

- Health

- Self-comparison

- Social environment

It's important to remember that self-esteem is one of those areas where we can redirect brain plasticity. We know that it isn't fixed and can be changed. You can even measure it. Start where you are. Build your self-esteem day by day and you'll start to see that's it's malleable and can be shaped and increased by your actions.

Increasing your self-esteem won't automatically make you better at everything. What it will do is motivate you, increase your overall wellbeing and enable you to flourish throughout your life.

Perhaps surprisingly, researchers have found that both high and low levels of self-esteem can present individual and social difficulties. High self-esteem doesn't necessarily result in healthy self-esteem. Research has shown that people with very high levels of self-esteem are more likely to blame others when they fail. They also have a higher frequency of aggression. For people with healthy self-esteem, the focus is different. They look at failures and attempt to find new ways of improving next time. So where should our self-esteem be? Positive self-esteem functions somewhere in the middle of the two and it tends to be healthier and more effective. Self-esteem expert Dr John Grohol designed six steps to increase it:

1. Audit your self-esteem to find your baseline. Grohol argues that you can't fix what you don't know needs fixing. He suggests taking a piece of paper and listing ten strengths and ten weaknesses to create an inventory of your self-esteem. You might discover that the weaknesses are easier to list, most of us do – but take your time, you'll find strengths if you try.

2. Set realistic goals. It's usual to look at a list of weaknesses and want to make huge, sweeping changes. If enormous change was so easy, we would have done it already. Think small, realistic goals and steadily build up to the bigger, more complex ones that you want to achieve.

3. Let go of perfectionism. The chance of any of us ever being perfect is pretty slim. It's unattainable. Grohol reiterates the point that the perfection we see in the media and online doesn't exist. It's carefully curated to present the illusion of perfection. Instead, he recommends grabbing hold of your achievements. Recognizing what you do well and have achieved instead of brushing it off. As you're grabbing hold of your accomplishments it's also important to pay attention to your failures. Mistakes are an opportunity for learning and growth.

4. Explore yourself. Self-exploration is an opportunity to look at all of the facets of your identity. As well as recognizing your strengths and weaknesses, this includes being open to new experiences. Expanding your outlook by trying new things, meeting new people and listening to different world views are all ways that you can explore yourself.

5. Be willing to adjust your self-image. We can get stuck in old, inaccurate perceptions about who we are and what we can achieve. As you grow, experience new things and work on yourself, it's important to adjust your self-image to match your ever-developing skills and abilities.

6. Stop comparing yourself to others. Self-comparison damages our self-esteem and just leads to feeling bad. Focus your energy on yourself and your personal growth instead.

USING POSITIVE AFFIRMATIONS ✦ & VISUALIZATIONS TO CREATE ✦ THE LIFE YOU WANT

Affirmations and visualizations have long been used as a strategy to improve performance in the sporting world. Scientists have examined the impact that positive affirmations have on the brain, finding that when positive affirmations are used consistently they help us to maintain positive self-perception. They also help us to combat negative self-thoughts. There is a caveat, though. People who don't believe the positive affirmations that they are using, such as 'I'm worthy of love' or 'I am my ideal weight', may end up feeling worse. It's important, then, to use affirmations that you feel you can work with, rather than resist and feel that they're not true.

It might be that we need a certain level of self-esteem for declarative affirmations to have a positive impact. For some of us, the old idiom 'fake it until you make it' just doesn't ring true. Psychologist Dan Pink cautions against self-talk that attempts to pump you up but feels empty. If you find that declarative affirmations like 'I am' or 'I will' don't work for you, you can try an alternative technique known as interrogative self-talk.

◆ INTERROGATIVE SELF-TALK ◆

While it is widely acknowledged that positive self-talk is better for us than negative self-talk, interrogative self-talk adds another layer. This technique involves asking yourself questions. It moves 'I will' to 'Will I?' and 'I am' to 'Am I?', with excellent results. For example, 'How am I going to reach my goal?' or, 'Am I willing to do this?' or, 'Can I do this?' You could break your goal down even further by asking, 'How can I do this?'

It may sound a little like self-doubt, but researchers found that the introduction of a question and an exploration of ability, focused on growth, created a deeper and lasting confidence.

· · · · · · · · · · ● ● ● ● ● ● ● · · · · · · · · · ·

Practical exercise

Things that are good about me

Write down twenty things that are good about you. You can use these sentences as prompts.

◀ *One thing about me that is unique is...* ▶

◀ *I make other people happy when I...* ▶

◀ *I'm good at...* ▶

◀ *I feel good about...* ▶

◀ *I'm proud of my...* ▶

◀ *I'm gifted at...* ▶

◀ *One thing I do well is...* ▶

· · · · · · · · · · · · ● ● ● ● ● · · · · · · · · · ·

◆ STOP COMPARING YOURSELF ◆

Stop comparing yourself. You're not in competition with anyone else. Known as self-referential processing, this can really hurt your self-esteem. Whether it's comparing upwards or downwards, research shows that it's detrimental to your wellbeing. If you're looking down on someone else and thinking, 'Thank goodness that's not me,' or up thinking, 'They're so successful and I'm nowhere near that good,' you're decreasing your level of happiness. The next time that you're tempted to compare your efforts, let go of perfectionism and practise self-acceptance instead.

◆ FLIP BACK, FLICK UP ◆

This is a technique where you flip back into a scenario where you were successful and felt confident.

- What was happening?

- What kind of self-talk did you use?

- How did you feel? What emotions were there for you? Were there any physical sensations?

- What did you do?

Now think of a situation in which you'd like to be more confident. Flick those positive emotions from the successful event into the new scenario and ask:

- How could you change your self-talk?

- What might help you to feel more confident?

- What emotions could you invoke?

- What can you do differently in the new situation?

▲▲▲

POSITIVITY
&
RELATIONSHIPS

WHY POSITIVE RELATIONSHIPS MATTER

So far, we've focused on developing a positive, healthy and supportive relationship with yourself. The reason? That's the cornerstone of positivity. While the relationship that we have with ourselves is one of the most important in life, who we surround ourselves with can be equally important.

Motivational speaker Jim Rohn maintained that when it comes to relationships, you are the average of the five people that you spend the most time with. Think about that for a moment. Who do you surround yourself with? How do you feel when you're in their company?

There are some relationships that deplete and drain you. You'll recognize them by the amount of energy that they take to maintain. If you're not sure whether a relationship is toxic, see how many of these statements characterize the relationship:

- You feel drained after spending time with them

- You don't feel supported

- It feels unequal, as though you're the one sustaining it

- The other person has a permanently negative narrative that permeates your dialogue together

- You feel 'less' than you did before being with them

- There is an imbalance of power in your relationship

- Thinking about them feels like an effort

Who we invite into our personal lives affects our mood, our motivation and our wellbeing. It also has an impact upon our health.

◆ TOXIC RELATIONSHIPS AND 'MOOD HOOVERS' ◆

A UK longitudinal study called Whitehall II has followed the health of 10,000 people since 1988. One of the areas that the researchers have examined is negative relationships. They asked each of the people in the study to classify their closest personal relationships as either negative or positive. The results were concerning.

Those people describing their close personal relationships as positive experienced reassurance, high self-esteem and demonstrable benefits for their overall wellbeing.

The people defining their closest relationships as negative fared less well. They experienced more stress, anxiety and depression than their counterparts with positive relationships. They were also more likely to experience Type 2 diabetes and cardiac health problems, including an increased risk of a fatal heart attack. That's a high price to pay for negative relationships.

What steps can you take if you recognize a negative relationship in your life and want to safeguard yourself?

- Ask yourself if you value this relationship enough to maintain it. Has it run its course? Without blame or judgement, would you really like to move on? If yes, it might be time to do so.

- Is it a family relationship or one with ties that you would rather not break? Consider limiting the amount of time that you spend with that person. Is there a way of keeping communication open without subjecting yourself to negativity? It may be that you decide upon a set amount of time that you are willing to spend in that person's company.

- If you are concerned about your personal safety in a negative relationship, it's important to reach out and get advice from professionals who can support you.

If you've been surrounded by a fog of negativity, it can be hard to differentiate between what's working for you and what isn't. You might also be wondering about what happens if you jettison all of your negative relationships, only to discover that there's no one left in your social circle. Making new friends is a lifelong habit that is well worth cultivating. Investing time in new friendships and experiences that move you out of your comfort zone is a major step that will support the practise of positivity throughout your life. We've taken a good look at what a negative relationship looks like, but what would you expect to see in a positive relationship?

◆ RELATIONSHIPS THAT ◆ SUPPORT YOU ...

- Are respectful. You respect each other and that is demonstrated in the language that you use and how you behave towards each other.

- Demonstrate empathy. You might not always agree with friends and family but you listen with empathy and attempt to see the world from their perspective.

- There is give and take. You both contribute equally to the relationship.

- You support each other when you need help and remember details about each other's lives.

- Your differences are celebrated and accepted.

- You trust each other.

- You feel able to discuss difficulties in a constructive way.

- When you listen you do so without judgement.

- You engage in life-affirming, healthy activities together.

All of these behaviours form a good baseline for developing positive relationships. Think of it as a checklist. If you recognize areas that you would like to work on, pick one item at a time and set yourself small, achievable goals in that area. For example, if you'd like to listen more to others, set a goal to allow them to finish speaking before you offer your thoughts. Or if you want to work on being non-judgemental, pause and consider the situation from the other person's perspective before you respond. You might also decide to use phrases that confer respect, such as, 'That's really interesting, I've never thought about it like that before,' instead of launching into a counterpoint or arguing for your own point of view.

· · · · · · · · · · · · · ● ● ● ● · · · · · · · · · ·

Practical exercise

Energy domains
It can be helpful to consider your energy within three domains:

You: your nutrition, sleep and opportunity for rest and renewal. These are all areas that are likely to be neglected.

Professional domain: we spend a lot of our time at work. This is about your work-life balance. What motivates you to work? Are your values aligned with what you do every day? Are you able to adequately refuel and take breaks throughout the day?

Social domain: this contains family, friends and other social relationships. If all of your energy is going into your professional domain, this area can suffer. Social connection is one of the most effective barriers against stress that we have, and it's important to maintain healthy relationships.

When we achieve balance across all three domains, our wellbeing, performance, productivity and happiness are optimized. It's the ability to maintain an energy equilibrium that develops resilience, helping us to bounce back when there are bumps in the road. Take a look at the three domains and where you place most of your energy. Are there areas that you would like to adjust?

····•• **DOMAIN 1** ••····

◀ *Do I invest time in myself?* ▶

◀ *Is there space for rest and renewal?* ▶

◀ *Do my nutritional habits
help or hinder my energy?* ▶

◀ *What is my sleep hygiene like?* ▶

◀ *Where is my downtime?* ▶

◦◦◦◦◦• **DOMAIN 2** •◦◦◦◦◦◦

◄ *What is my motivation for work?* ►

◄ *Do I live and work in alignment with my values?* ►

◄ *Am I able to be my authentic self?* ►

◄ *Do I have a purpose?* ►

◄ *Do I take regular breaks?* ►

◄ *How do I refuel at work?* ►

◄ *Am I able to manage my time and energy in a way that works for me?* ►

◄ *Do I need to create stronger boundaries or say no more often?* ►

······• DOMAIN 3 •······

Do I sacrifice all of my
◄ *energy at work with nothing left* ►
for myself afterwards?

◄ *Where can I create more time* ►
for positive relationships?

Are there areas where
◄ *I want to limit my time around* ►
toxic relationships?

Are there old relationships
◄ *or friendships that I would* ►
like to reconnect with?

▲▲▲

GRATITUDE

Gratitude, not surprisingly, is good for us; but just what is it? Gratitude researchers Robert Emmons and Michael McCullough have broken the emotion of gratitude down into a two-stage process:

- Identifying that there has been a positive outcome

- Recognizing that there is an external source for that positive outcome

Gratitude can be towards other people, nature, health, enjoyable moments or a higher power. Broadly speaking, psychologists break gratitude down into three types:

Affective trait: this is your overall disposition towards gratitude or how grateful you typically are.

Emotion: the temporary feeling of gratitude that we experience, for example, after something good happens, or when you share a pleasant time with someone.

Mood: this is the fluctuation of gratitude that you experience throughout the day.

◆ THE SCIENCE OF GRATITUDE ◆

When we search for things to be grateful for every day, we are actively seeking out the positive. This one simple act begins to rewire our brain, moving away from focusing on what is wrong and what isn't working towards the things that are. Research by psychologist Martin Seligman found that experiencing gratitude daily was consistently linked to decreased depression, greater happiness, health, optimism and wellbeing. One study even found that people who were grateful had fewer biomarkers of cellular inflammation in their body than those who were not.

◆ YOUR MIND ON GRATITUDE ◆

Research from one of the world's leading experts in positive emotions, Professor Barbara Fredrickson, suggests that they can be built. Her theory, known as 'Broaden and Build', demonstrates how positive emotions can help us flourish in personal relationships, in the workplace as leaders or employees. Good emotions even impact positively upon our longevity. Barbara Fredrickson agrees that gratitude is beneficial. Her 'Broaden and Build' theory that we can broaden our thoughts and actions with positive emotions includes the act of gratitude. It may even cancel out some of our more negative emotions.

Many studies have found that gratitude is linked to psychological wellbeing as well as increased physical health. Gratitude may provide protective health benefits for those who practise it. When we're grateful, our life satisfaction increases and we become less materialistic and less likely to compare ourselves to others. Gratitude makes us more prosocial, kind and generous to others. We're also less likely to burn out at work.

▲▲▲

GRATITUDE, ANXIETY AND DEPRESSION

It is often posited that gratitude may undo some of the causes of everyday unhappiness. Gratitude provides us with a useful way of reframing negative events. It also reduces the amount of attention that we pay to negative information.

Scientists tell us that gratitude can move our thinking from negative to positive, alleviating depression. Our brains become flooded with oxytocin, serotonin and dopamine, the feel-good hormones. As a result, we feel increased efficacy, more confident and better able to manage negative events.

BARRIERS TO GRATITUDE

There are some activities that we engage in that can become barriers to gratitude. These include cynicism, narcissism, self-comparison, materialism and envy. One of the reasons for this may be because when we experience these emotions we

73

are focusing on what we do not have, rather than what we do. We're coming from a place of deficit and that never feels good. Intentionally looking for and expressing gratitude is one way to overcome these barriers.

◆ CULTIVATING THE ◆ GRATITUDE HABIT

You can increase your level of gratitude by intentionally engaging in gratitude every day. When you recognize the goodness in your life, you begin to increase gratitude. Positive psychology studies have consistently linked gratitude to greater happiness. Gratitude can be expressed in many ways. Whatever your current level of gratitude, you can always cultivate more with the interventions outlined in the practical exercises section.

▲▲▲

* *

Practical exercise

Gratitude journal

Each day write down five things that you are grateful for. Notice the difference as you do this over a period of time. You can modify this to a gratitude conversation every day with a friend, partner, sibling or child to develop the habit of gratitude. You'll be helping the person that you're communicating with too.

Three good things

This is a variation of the gratitude journal. Write down three things that have gone well for you each day. With three good things, you also identify the causes of those good events.

Gratitude email or text

Send a message to someone who you are grateful to. Email or text them to express gratitude and say thank you. Not only will you be making someone else's day, but studies show that you'll be increasing your own happiness levels, too.

Mental subtraction

This involves imagining what your life would be like if a positive event had not occurred. This is known as the 'George Bailey effect', after the protagonist in the classic movie *It's a Wonderful Life*. It will help you to get perspective on the things that already exist in your life.

Recalling gratitude

Scientists have discovered that recalling positive events from the past that you are grateful for will increase your happiness levels. This is especially useful if you are struggling for gratitude on a difficult day. Create a record of significant positive events that you can draw upon and recall in times of difficulty. Go back as far as you need to and vividly describe them as you write. You could record these positive events on cue cards, Post-it notes, pieces of paper in a jar or in a dedicated recall notebook. Whichever you choose becomes your go-to place on days when gratitude feels in short supply.

Kindness counting

Count the number of acts of kindness that you do every day. This has the added benefit of making kindness a more intentional routine in your daily activity.

▲▲▲

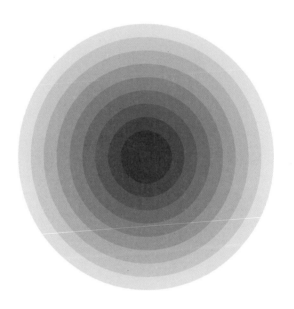

TAKING
CONTROL
of your
DIGITAL
WELLBEING

▼▼▼

Social media can connect us and facilitate learning. It provides many, many benefits, but there's also a downside. Studies suggest that constant connection can leave us feeling drained, depleted and socially isolated. It's an unfortunate unintended consequence of using technology.

If you feel jittery at the thought of being separated from your device, there's a name for it: nomophobia. It's the fear and anxiety that you experience when you are separated from your phone. It's not just our phones – our increased reliance on and use of gadgets has been found to negatively impact our mental health, focus and sleep.

Researchers investigating the impact of digital connection found evidence that, since 2000, the use of technology has reduced our attention span from twelve to eight seconds. There is also a suggestion that use of social media by children has prevented the development of communication skills and the ability to read social cues when face-to-face.

A study from Texas University suggests that it's how we use social media that's the problem, rather than social media itself. As with pretty much everything in life, there is nothing inherently harmful in the digital world. It's how we use it that creates problems.

As a population, we're far more connected than we've ever been. When we're constantly on social media, our attention span diminishes and we're less likely to notice habits that may be detrimental. How do we know when it's time to reconsider how we interact with our technology?

◆ DIGITAL RESILIENCE ◆

Think about how you use all of your digital devices. Are you constantly connected? Do you notice that when you have a spare moment, you're tempted to reach for your phone? Does the thought of minimizing your use of technology leave you feeling defensive? These are all clues that it might be time to rethink how you are interacting with your technology. Constant connection can drain our energy and diminish our focus on real-world tasks. Bringing awareness of how you use technology and creating a more balanced approach is the key to mastering your digital resilience.

◆ WHY TOO MUCH TECH ◆ WILL DEPRESS YOU

Researchers are beginning to ask if technology can cause anxiety and depression. The evidence seems to be growing that there is a link between social media and depression. Some studies have found a correlation between low mood, depression and the use of social media platforms. A 2015 study by the University of Missouri suggested that using Facebook results in a negative mood shift. That's bad news for positivity. Studies suggest that it seems likely that heavy social media use exacerbates existing mental health conditions, including depression and anxiety. Whether technology is at fault is a debate that is likely to continue.

Anxiety is characterized by worried thoughts, tension and physiological symptoms including increased heart rate and an elevation in blood pressure. It's an emotion that we'll all experience at some point. For most people, it subsides. Social media can sometimes feed into it. If you recognize a connection between your use of social media and anxiety it could be time to consider managing this more closely.

◆ MANAGING SOCIAL MEDIA ◆

There is a great deal of discussion around addiction and technology. One of the biggest culprits is our smartphone. It's always so accessible, it's no wonder that in our spare moments, it's usually the first thing we reach for. Managing your social media and being more intentional in your use of it will help you to cultivate more positivity.

▲▲▲

◆ THE BENEFITS ◆
OF UNPLUGGING

While unplugging might feel like a nuclear option for some of us, there are clear benefits of creating digital downtime within your day. Digital information overload can result in a state where we're constantly on alert. This phenomenon is sometimes referred to as novelty addiction. The pace when we stop feels slow and stagnant. We fill that gap by reaching for further connection with technology, strengthening the cycle, creating 'popcorn brain'. This is the state where our brain becomes used to being immersed in the digital world with the constant, rapid 'popping' of stimulation at a pace that real life doesn't or can't always emulate. When we're connected we're only a swipe away from our next hit of dopamine. It's not sustainable and can become problematic in the real world where there is less obvious opportunity for an easy, feel-good dopamine hit.

▲▲▲

Practical exercise

If you recognize that you're spending excessive time on social media and decide it's time to create some digital downtime in your day, here are six steps that will help you to achieve more balance.

1. Audit your devices. Create a list, then decide how much time you want to spend on each one and schedule it into your day. This will help you prevent 'tech drift' – when you go online for 'five' minutes and it turns into fifty.

2. Be realistic. Eliminating technology from your life is probably not practical. Bring intentionality to your digital usage. Think about when you absolutely need (or want) to use it and when you are more easily able to switch off.

3. Delete digital applications. If your apps aren't easily available, you'll be less tempted to reach

for them. The same is true with alerts and notifications. Turn them off.

4. Think about how you use technology at different times of your day. If you eat while using gadgets (including the TV), see if it's possible to introduce device-free meal times.

5. To prevent 'device creep' in work meetings, phone-stack. This is where everyone places their phone in the middle of the table, just out of reach. This makes the furtive gadget-check more tricky – no one wants to be the first to reach into the middle of the pile.

6. If your day starts with the alarm on your phone, think about a clockwork alarm instead. It may seem old-fashioned, but you won't be tempted to check emails, news and social media as soon as you wake up. Leave your phone in a different room and use the time you would have spent scrolling on a task that develops your positivity instead.

▲▲▲

SELF-CARE
&
COMPASSION

◆ SELF-CARE AND RENEWAL ◆

We can often be so busy looking after other people that we forget to take care of ourselves. There is a saying that you cannot pour from an empty cup. Self-care isn't selfish or self-indulgent. It's one of the most pragmatic things that you can do to help others. Unless you make time to care for yourself it is difficult to support and be there for anyone else.

◆ SELF-COMPASSION ◆

There are many competing definitions of compassion. It isn't sympathy or empathy; compassion is more than that. Compassion is noticing someone's suffering, feeling sympathy and then doing something to help them.

Kristin Neff, one of the world's leading researchers into compassion, divides it into three key components:

1. **Self-kindness vs self-judgement. We reduce our self-judgement and self-blame, replacing**

it with self-kindness. There is an acceptance of ourselves that is absent when we lack self-compassion.

2. Mindfulness vs over-identification with thoughts. We begin to recognize that thoughts are just thoughts. They don't represent reality. When we are able to bring awareness to our thoughts, we are better able to manage them.

3. Common humanity vs isolation. When we acknowledge our common humanity and connection we realize that we're not separate from each other. Being able to identify that we're all human beings experiencing the same challenges, the same emotions and the same difficulties helps us to foster compassion for both ourselves and others.

Developing self-compassion can help us to be kinder to ourselves. It can dial down the volume of our inner critic. Studies consistently link self-compassion to wellbeing and resilience. When we're kinder to ourselves we can manage the ups and downs of life more skilfully. Regular practise of self-compassion has been linked to:

- Greater happiness

- Increased resilience

- Improved self-regulation

- Reduced anxiety and depression

- A decrease in comparing ourselves to others

- Silencing negative self-talk

◆ COMPASSION BACKDRAFT ◆

One thing that you might not expect when you begin to practise greater self-compassion towards yourself is something called compassion backdraft. This happens when all of the things that you were feeling bad about, at first, begin to feel worse. This sometimes happens when we begin to examine things that we've buried deep down or previously avoided. There's nothing wrong with you if you notice this. Once we begin looking at problems or negative memories, they can appear to be amplified. If you experience this, remember it's always okay to stop if you feel overwhelmed. Making sure that you look after yourself and do only what feels comfortable; this is part of being compassionate towards yourself.

COMPASSION TOWARDS OTHERS

In the same way that self-compassion increases positivity, compassion towards others brings enormous benefits. Dacher Keltner, a professor of psychology at the University of California, describes compassion as 'an evolved part of human nature, rooted in our brain and biology'. For some people, that might sound counterintuitive in a society that encourages competition. For years, psychology has attempted to examine human behaviour from the perspective of what is wrong. Examining what works and serves us as human beings is a different approach. There have been many studies that suggest compassion is essential for the human race to survive. If we take a look at studies into the animal kingdom, we can see that even rodents exhibit empathy and will avoid harming other rats. A study in the journal *Current Biology* demonstrated this 'harm aversion' trait when rats would not pull a lever that delivered a mild electric shock to another rat. Christian Keysers, of the Netherlands Institute for Neuroscience and one of the authors of the study, suggests that harm aversion may be evolutionarily 'hardwired' into mammals.

Acts of compassion have benefits for our health and wellbeing. UCLA researchers discovered that people living a life which they described as full of 'purpose and meaning', focusing on helping others, had low inflammation levels in their body. The opposite is true for those who described the source of their happiness as 'pleasure' alone.

▲▲▲

◆ THE POWER OF KINDNESS ◆

Kindness means that you give something of yourself to someone else. From small, micro acts of kindness to grand gestures, we're doing something for someone else. We sometimes underestimate the power of kindness. Even in situations where kindness may seem counterintuitive, for example in the military, researchers have found that it provides a competitive advantage. Wallace Bachman's work, 'Nice Guys Finish First', analyzing naval commanders, found that commanders with high levels of emotional intelligence inspired increased motivation and performance in their team. Kindness is a powerful quality that provides science-backed benefits for the giver and the receiver.

◆ THE SCIENCE OF KINDNESS ◆

When we engage in kindness, studies demonstrate that we experience an increase in oxytocin, better known as the 'love hormone', along with serotonin, the 'happiness hormone'. The associated benefits of these hormones in the body include lowered blood pressure, increased optimism, improved heart health, greater self-esteem and self-efficacy. There are even neurological benefits provided by the neuroplasticity that takes place when you behave kindly.

A study at Harvard Business School across 136 countries found that people who were more financially generous were the happiest. It wasn't the amount that mattered, it was the act of giving, of being kind. Whether you're the giver or receiver of kindness, you'll still experience the benefits of oxytocin. All great reasons to make kindness one of your daily habits.

Kindness isn't limited to making you feel good. It has a profound effect on our physical health. Scientists have also discovered that people who engage in regular acts of kindness have 23% less of the stress hormone cortisol in their bodies. They also age less rapidly. Kindness is a quick win in terms of your positivity.

MINFULNESS AND KIND-FULNESS

◆ MINDFULNESS AND ◆
KIND-FULNESS

Mindfulness is a meditative practice focusing on paying attention to the present moment without judging what happens. Think of it as a way of training your brain. Researchers have demonstrated that practising mindfulness on a regular basis reduces stress and depression and increases neuroplasticity, with many regular meditators reporting feeling happier.

Practical exercise

Sixty seconds of mindfulness

Pause for a moment and focus on your breath. See if it's possible to follow your breath all the way in from the tip of your nostrils, into your nasal cavities, down into your lungs and out again. Notice each in-breath and each out-breath as best you can for sixty seconds. If your mind wanders and you begin to drift off into thoughts, gently escort your focus back to your breath. Congratulations, you've just completed sixty seconds of mindfulness.

Developing 'metta'

There is emerging evidence to suggest that specific mindfulness practices can lead to prosocial (kind) behaviour. One of these is the loving-kindness meditation, sometimes called a 'metta' meditation. It consists of repeating a series of phrases (or mantras) to yourself. Sometimes when we try to develop kindness (and compassion) we can feel resistance to it. There might be people that you don't want to direct kindness to and that's okay. Begin where you are and only do what you feel comfortable with. This meditation shouldn't feel forced. Try to allow the feelings of kindness to emerge naturally. You can also change the phrasing to make sure that it feels right for you.

Get into a comfortable position.

With the loving-kindness meditation, it's usual to begin by sending kindness to yourself. Say to yourself:

· · · ● ●

May I be safe. May I be well.
May I be happy. May I be loved.

● ● ● · ·

Rest as you say each phrase. You do not need to try to force feelings of kindness. Notice whatever feelings come and go without judging them.

Now, if it feels right for you, think of someone who you have positive feelings towards. Say to yourself:

· · · ● ●

May you be safe. May you be well.
May you be happy. May you be loved.

● ● ● · ·

Again, as you say this, notice the feelings that arise towards this person who is dear to you.

Now choose someone who you have neutral feelings towards.

· · · · ●

May you be safe. May you be well.
May you be happy. May you be loved.

● · · · ·

Finally, and only if it feels comfortable for you, choose someone who you have difficulty with. It's also okay to completely skip this section.

· · · ● ●

May you be safe. May you be well.
May you be happy. May you be loved.

● · · · ·

If you notice difficulty as you say this, don't judge it; see if it's possible to observe it and allow it to subside. If it becomes too difficult, stop – remember to extend self-compassion towards yourself. You can always choose someone who feels easier to work with for this section.

Everyday kindness

Think of ways that you could incorporate more kindness into your day. Where are the opportunities with friends, family, at work or with strangers? How can you go out of your way to be kinder to others?

Being kind to yourself

It takes time to develop self-compassion. A good place to begin is by setting an intention every day to be more compassionate to yourself.

If you encounter difficulty during the day, press pause and give yourself a self-compassion break. It doesn't need to be hours – sixty seconds is enough if that's all you have. Take deep breaths and ask yourself what you need right now to move forwards with compassion for yourself and others.

Journalling

Try journalling. Writing regularly has been linked to improved wellbeing. See if it's possible to write about any areas that you are struggling with. Sometimes, just writing things down is enough to get things out. Reflect on your journal entries with love and compassion. Imagine that you are reading them and responding as you would to a good friend, with love, non-judgement and compassion.

RANDOM ACTS OF KINDNESS (RAKs)

Random acts of kindness are moments in the day when you intentionally do something kind for someone else. You can sprinkle kindness throughout your day by:

1. Texting friends or family a message of positivity.

2. If you buy a morning coffee, paying for the coffee of the person behind you – otherwise known as paying it forward.

3. Donating clothes or household items that you no longer use to charity.

4. Giving up your seat on public transport.

5. Smiling at a stranger.

6. Sending an email to a colleague letting them know how grateful you are for their work.

7. Holding a door open for someone.

8. Connecting someone in your network with someone else you know, supporting their development.

9. Telling you friends or family how much you appreciate them.

10. Paying someone a compliment.

▲▲▲

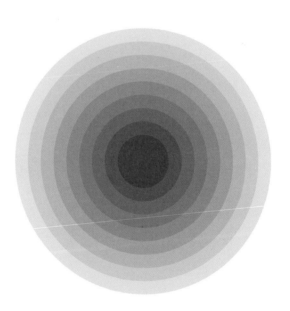

DEVELOPING
RESILIENCE

Think about resilience and what springs to mind? You'll hear people referring to resilience as 'bouncing back'. The analogy of a ball is a useful one. The ball may fall, it might it get squashed on the way down, changing its shape, but it bounces back up again to its original form.

The ball presents us with a useful image to build upon. Resilience is more complex than bouncing back from failure, trauma or difficulty. It's the ability to adapt and thrive during difficult times. Resilience is our ability to manage stressful life events successfully.

That doesn't mean that you won't ever have moments of despair, or moments where you feel down. It's what you do with those moments when life is difficult that makes the difference.

While there is evidence that factors such as genetics, our life experiences and luck affect our resilience, we can still learn to be more resilient. Making time to develop your emotional resilience will help you to adapt and deal with trauma, tragedy, stress, pressure and the curveballs that come your way in life.

◆ STRESS PERCEPTION ◆

Our perception of stress has an impact on how able we feel to manage it. If we see stress as a challenge, as something to master, we can be energized by it. If, however, when you experience stress you perceive it as overwhelming, as insurmountable, this creates an anxious and unhelpful response that can paralyze you. If you are able to shift your perception of stress to one that is energized when adverse events present themselves, you'll feel better able to manage them.

Try creating some positive stress response phrases to help you achieve a perception of challenge rather than overwhelm. Use your own phrases that resonate with you. Here are some suggestions.

◄ *I am energized by stress.* ►

◄ *This is good for my brain and is propelling me into action.* ►

◄ *I've dealt successfully with stress in the past and I can deal with this.* ►

CONSISTENT HABITS

The habits that we consistently practise can all count towards building our resilience. When you ensure that you get adequate sleep, eat a balanced and healthy diet and exercise daily, you'll find that you are better placed to manage challenges that come your way. These might sound obvious steps to resilience, but when we're stressed, they're often the first things that we neglect. Think of this as prioritizing your energy levels and self-care.

▲▲▲

◆ THE PERMA MODEL ◆

PERMA is a wellbeing model designed by positive psychologist Martin Seligman. It sets out five core components necessary for wellbeing and happiness. Think of the five components as building blocks for happiness and resilience. The five elements of PERMA are:

Positive emotions

Positive emotions go beyond feeling happy. They include love, gratitude, compassion, contentment, zest, joy, hope and amusement. Here are some practices that will help you build those life-enhancing emotions.

- Random acts of kindness.

- Make sure you carve out time for people who are important to you.

- Build a resilience circle: friends who energize and renew you when you are with them. Leave the emotional vampires at home for this one.

Engagement

Seligman describes engagement as 'being one with the music, time stopping, and the loss of self-consciousness during an absorbing activity'. You might know this state as 'flow'. We lose track of time in flow. Moments pass imperceptibly, hours can feel like minutes. When you are in flow you are also experiencing a stretch in your skills, focusing on something that provides you with a challenge.

Professor Mihaly Csikszentmihalyi, author of *Flow*, is the leading authority on this topic. He describes how the intense concentration of flow is energizing, satisfying and contributes to our overall wellbeing. Csikszentmihalyi proposes that it is possible to increase our level of happiness by introducing more flow. Here are some ways to develop engagement:

- Practise mindfulness techniques to limit distractions and increase your focus on the present moment (one of the conditions necessary for flow).

- Savour being in the moment, noticing how you are feeling and what you are thinking along with any associated bodily sensations.

- Identify your strengths. Take Seligman and Peterson's free VIA Character Strengths Assessment (go to www.authentic-happiness.com). Seligman and Csikszentmihalyi agree that using your strengths will increase your happiness and positive emotions and facilitate flow.

Relationships

The third component of the PERMA model is relationships. Seligman states that we are social creatures, and that positive relationships have a significant impact on our wellbeing.

Relationships expert Shelly Gable describes how sharing positive news with others enhances our relationships. Gable also studied couples and found those who communicated and responded enthusiastically to each other (active-constructive responding, as Gable termed it) experienced greater wellbeing. Building and maintaining your social network may also protect you against cognitive decline.

How can you build your social network?

- Go to new places and engage in new activities

- Be interested in other people

- Develop your listening skills

- Join a class or take up a hobby

- Re-establish relationships with people that you have lost touch with

- Create time to see friends and maintain your current relationships

- Be positive: people enjoy being around others who energize them

Meaning

Seligman describes meaning as something greater than ourselves. Meaning comes in many forms; it's your purpose for being on the planet. Perhaps it's a cause you feel strongly about; it could be your work or pursuing an activity that you feel you were placed upon the earth to do. Finding meaning is often linked to values that you hold dear, something important to you. Research in this area indicates that people with a purpose live longer, are more likely to experience personal growth after trauma and enjoy increased wellbeing. Purpose isn't found in possessions or constant busyness: it takes place at a much deeper level.

- Consider supporting an organization that you care about.

- Spend time reflecting upon your values. Can you identify a top ten? Your values will act as your guide when it comes to life, purpose and goal setting so it's worth setting aside time to identify what they are.

- Develop your authenticity. Accept your flaws and become the best version of yourself.

- Do something for someone else on a regular

basis. We know that meaning is a lifelong pursuit, so devote time to it – the evidence suggests every now and again is of little benefit. Consistency is important.

Accomplishment

The final element of the PERMA model of wellbeing is accomplishment, or 'I did it, and I did it well', as Seligman puts it. Accomplishment requires setting goals, and mastery of those goals.

We know that achieving goals, especially those linked to your values, increases wellbeing over a period of time. Goals motivate us and help us to develop a growth mindset, a belief that we can try new things and succeed (even if it takes a while).

- The obvious starting point is setting goals. You're more likely to achieve them if they're SMART (specific, measurable, achievable, realistic and time-bound).

- Set yourself small goals to begin with and build up to larger goals. Think of them as goal reps just like you would with weights at the gym.

- Celebrate and savour your achievements.

- If goals really aren't your thing, consider making changes to your current habits: small incremental steps will pay dividends. For example, if you want to increase your physical fitness and you catch the bus to work every day, consider getting off a stop early to increase your steps. Tiny tweaks will make a big difference.

* * *

Practical exercise

Audit each of the areas of the PERMA model. Use the prompts of each component to work out where you would like to create changes.

* * *

▲▲▲

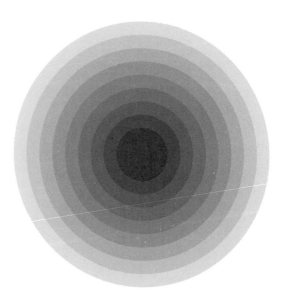

GROWTH
MINDSET

Professor Carol Dweck has been researching the concept of mindset for the last thirty-five years. Arguably, mindset sits at the core of a life filled with positivity. Mindset shapes our life on a daily basis. Dweck identified two types of mindset: fixed and growth.

Fixed mindset

This is the belief that talent and intelligence are set in stone. You believe that talent creates success. With a fixed mindset you don't believe that hard work and effort will make a difference, so you don't try to change things. Worse still, you mistakenly believe that if you try and fail, others will think that you're foolish. With this mindset, failure is all-defining.

Growth mindset

With a growth mindset, brains and talent are the starting point. You recognize that success takes effort. You can learn and improve – with effort. You learn from your failures and recognize this as the process of mastery.

Rather than being completely growth or fixed mindset, you'll probably find that you are a mixture of both. Think of it as a continuum. In some areas of life, you may have a growth mindset, in others, fixed.

◆ DEVELOPING A
GROWTH MINDSET ◆

Perhaps you've recognized that you have a fixed mindset in some areas of your life? Dweck recommends a four-stage process to building a growth mindset.

Stage 1:

Learn to identify your fixed mindset inner dialogue voice

'You'll fail.' 'People will think I'm stupid if I can't do it.' 'You're no good at this.' That self-talk is different for all of us. Listen out for it and tune into it. Recognizing that it's there is the first step to changing it.

Stage 2:

Realize that you have a choice

How you respond to hurdles, failures, setbacks and criticism is your choice. When you recognize this, you'll also be increasing your internal locus of control.

Stage 3:

Talk back to your negative dialogue with a growth mindset voice

'If I never try, I'll fail anyway.' 'All successful people have failed at some point and then succeeded.' 'If I fail, I'll learn from it and keep moving forwards.'

Stage 4:

Choose to act with a growth mindset approach in any given situation

1. View challenges as opportunities. Embrace them.

2. Learn from setbacks and try again, using what you learn from each failure.

3. Listen to feedback and criticism and use it to do things differently. Reframe criticism as 'information': a positive that will help you to be more successful.

4. View failure as a vehicle for learning.

5. Enjoy the process of learning. Reflect on a regular basis and recognize that you are training your brain each time you try something new.

6. Introduce the word 'yet' into your vocabulary. Dweck says this is one of her favourite words. When you don't succeed, remind yourself that you're on your way. Acknowledge that you haven't mastered that skill 'yet'.

Learning goals

Set yourself learning goals and apply the growth mindset principles to each goal. Reflect regularly on each goal and your progress.

Learn from failure

When you set a goal and things don't turn out as you had planned, examine what went wrong. What worked? What can you learn from what happened? How could you approach things differently next time?

▲▲▲

SUPPORTING
RESOURCES

ACCESSING THE POWER OF POSITIVITY

Positive Psychology in Practice.
www.health.harvard.edu/mind-and-mood/positive_
psychology_in_practice

Optimism, Cynical Hostility, and Incident Coronary Heart
Disease and Mortality in the Women's Health Initiative.
www.ahajournals.org/doi/full/10.1161/circulationaha.108.82
7642

Achor, S., *The Happiness Advantage*. Virgin Books, 2011.

REWIRING YOUR BRAIN FOR POSITIVITY

Fredrickson, B., Positive Emotions Open Our Mind.
ed.ted.com/on/MsjdksQK

Gilbert, D., The surprising science of happiness.
www.ted.com/talks/dan_gilbert_the_surprising_science_of_
happiness

Hanson, R., How to Hardwire Your Brain for Happiness!
'Buddha's Brain', Positive Psychology.
www.youtube.com/watch?v=4_tfR3bJPPM

How Positive Emotions Work and Why.
www.youtube.com/watch?v=nD_SbilNMo4

MASTERING NEGATIVE THOUGHTS

Ledgerwood, A., Getting stuck in the negatives (and how to get unstuck), TEDxUCDavis.
www.youtube.com/watch?v=7XFLTDQ4JMk

Gratitude and Well-being.
emmons.faculty.ucdavis.edu/gratitude-and-well-being/

USING POSITIVITY TO BUILD CONFIDENCE AND SELF-BELIEF

Falk, E. B. et al., Self-affirmation alters the brain's response to health messages and subsequent behaviour change, PNAS, 112(7), 2015.
www.ncbi.nlm.nih.gov/pmc/articles/PMC4343089/

Pink, D., Pinkcast 1.9. Pump yourself up... with a question.
www.danpink.com/pinkcast/pinkcast-1-9-pump-yourself-up-with-a-question/

Motivating goal-directed behavior through introspective self-talk: the role of the interrogative form of simple future tense.
www.ncbi.nlm.nih.gov/pubmed/20424090

POSITIVITY & RELATIONSHIPS

Ducharme, J., How to Tell If You're In a Toxic Relationship — And What To Do About It.
time.com/5274206/toxic-relationship-signs-help/

Hood, K., The difference between healthy and unhealthy love.
www.ted.com/talks/katie_hood_the_difference_between_healthy_and_unhealthy_love/transcript?language=en

Roffey, S., *Positive Relationships: Evidence-Based Practice across the World*. Springer, 2012.

Negative Aspects of Close Relationships as a Predictor of Increased Body Mass Index and Waist Circumference: The Whitehall II Study.
www.ncbi.nlm.nih.gov/pmc/articles/PMC3134502/

GRATITUDE

Steindl-Rast, D., Want to be happy? Be grateful.
www.ted.com/talks/david_steindl_rast_want_to_be_happy_be_grateful?language=en

Sarner, M., Is gratitude the secret of happiness?
www.theguardian.com/lifeandstyle/2018/oct/23/is-gratitude-secret-of-happiness-i-spent-month-finding-out

Wong, J. and Brown, J., How gratitude changes you and your brain.
greatergood.berkeley.edu/article/item/how_gratitude_
changes_you_and_your_brain

Your 5 day gratitude challenge
ideas.ted.com/your-5-day-gratitude-challenge-from-ted/

TAKING CONTROL OF YOUR
DIGITAL WELLBEING

Gordon, B., Social media is harmful to your brain and
relationships.
www.psychologytoday.com/us/blog/obesely-
speaking/201710/social-media-is-harmful-your-brain-and-
relationships

McSpadden, K., You Now Have a Shorter Attention Span
Than a Goldfish.
time.com/3858309/attention-spans-goldfish/

Newport, F., Most U.S. Smartphone Owners Check Phone
at Least Hourly.
news.gallup.com/poll/184046/smartphone-owners-check-
phone-least-hourly.aspx

SELF-CARE AND COMPASSION

Germer, C. K., *The mindful path to self-compassion: Freeing yourself from destructive thoughts and emotions.* New York: Guilford Press, 2009.

Gilbert, P. and Procter, S., Compassionate mind training for people with high shame and self-criticism: Overview and pilot study of a group therapy approach. Clinical Psychology and Psychotherapy 13, 353–379, 2006. doi:10.100/cpp.507

Neff, K., *Self-Compassion*. Yellow Kite, 2011.

Act With Compassion
www.actwithcompassion.com/therapist_resources

The Compassionate Mind Foundation
www.compassionatemind.co.uk/resources

DEVELOPING RESILIENCE

Brown, B., *Rising Strong*. Vermillion, 2015.

Brown, B., The Power of Vulnerability, RSA Talks.
www.youtube.com/watch?v=sXSjc-pbXk4&list=PLmvK0QBfWqL2G5B2vRIK3kgRO6P47Mm1u&index=5

Rose, R., How failure cultivates resilience.
www.ted.com/talks/raphael_rose_how_failure_cultivates_
resilience

The 10 best resilience videos
positivechangeguru.com/the-10-best-resilience-videos/

GROWTH MINDSET

Dweck, C., *Mindset. Updated Edition: Changing the way you think to fulfil your potential.* Robinson; 6th edition, 2017.

Dweck, C., The power of yet, TEDxNorrköping
www.youtube.com/watch?v=J-swZaKN2Ic

▲▲▲

ABOUT THE AUTHOR

Gill Thackray has lived and worked around the world as a performance psychologist, coach, consultant and trainer. She now lives in the Lake District in the UK and when not there, spends as much time as possible in Paris. She has been a visitor and sometimes resident of the same street, Rue Ordener in Montmartre, for the last twenty years. In her spare time, she writes about the history of the street and the 18th arrondissement of Paris at 'Zen and the Art of Being in Paris'.

You can find Gill at:

www.korudevelopment.com
Twitter @KoruDevelopment
Instagram @korudevelopment
www.zenandtheartofbeinginparis.com

▲▲▲